# Horses

## Children's Nature Library

GALLERY BOOKS
An Imprint of W. H. Smith Publishers Inc.

8 7 6 5 4 3 2 1

ISBN 0-8317-6471-6

This edition published in 1991 by Gallery
Books, an imprint of W.H. Smith Publishers,
Inc., 112 Madison Avenue, New York, New York
10016.

Gallery Books are available for bulk purchase
for sales and promotions and premium use.
For details write or telephone the Manager of
Special Sales, W.H. Smith Publishers, Inc.,
112 Madison Avenue, New York, New York
10016; (212) 532-6600.

Written by Eileen Spinelli

Credits:
Animals/Animals: Roger & Donna Aitkenhead:
57; Henry Ausloos: 13, 17, 20, 49, 50; Norvia
Behling: Front Cover, 1; George R. Cassidy: 41;
Margot Conte: 19, 36; Jerry Cooke: 8, 24, 37;
Harry Cutting: 36; E.R. Degginger: 10, 25, 26,
62; Henry R. Fox: 60; George R. Godfrey: 42;
Michael Habicht: 14; Richard Kolar: 15, 34;
Jane Langdon: 38; Zig Leszczynski: 7, 28, 60;
Bates Littlehales: 63; Robert Maier: 3, 12, 18,
20, 22, 23, 31, 32, 33, 45, 48, 52, 53, 54, 55,
64; Joe McDonald: 61; Stefan Meyers: 12; Patti
Murray: 60; Wendy Neefus: 30; Alan G. Nelson:
20; Robert Pearcy: 29; John L. Pontier: 27; Fritz
Prenzel: 21; Michael & Barbara Reed: 44, 47;
Ralph A. Reinhold: 10, 30, 39, 43, 44; Bradley
Smith: 46; Michael R. Stoklos: 40; Alfred B.
Thomas: 58, 59; Karen Tweedy-Holmes: 38;
Fred Whitehead: 40; Field Museum Of Natural
History: 4; FPG International: A. Schmidecker:
11, 51; George W. Hornal: 10; International
Stock Photography, Ltd.: 34; George Ancona:
26; Steve Behal: 8; Buzz Binzen: 9, 14, 16, 50;
Chad Ehlers: 24; Tom & Michele Grimm: 6, 34;
Ronn Maratea: 22; Robert W. Slack: 26, 40; Bill
Stanton: 35; Steve Kaufman: 56; Metro-
Goldwyn-Mayer, Inc.: 5; Yogi: R.Y. Kaufman: 4.

# Table of Contents

# History of Horses

Horse ancestors

Greek statue

Horses pulling a bus

Millions of years ago, an animal no bigger than a fox roamed the woods of North America. It evolved into a horse. Early humans painted these early horses on the walls of ancient caves.

The early Egyptians were afraid of horses. They may have used them to pull chariots, but they never rode on the horse's back! In ancient Greece, only the richest people owned horses. In Roman times, chariot races were popular. Racetracks in early Rome were called "circuses."

Christopher Columbus brought the horse to America. Horses helped develop the country by pulling plows and covered wagons, stagecoaches and fire engines, buses and milk trucks.

Horses pulling a chariot in a race ▶

# Horse Intelligence
# & Behavior

Horses are smart. Farm horses quickly learn chores. Show horses learn delightful routines. Horses have good memories. Many horses have a sense of humor.

Each horse is different. Some horses are gentle, some are rough. Some horses are easy to handle, some are stubborn. There are lazy horses and horses that work hard. Horses are usually good-natured. If a horse is in danger it runs away.

# Horse Intelligence & Behavior

Horses "talk" with whinny and neigh sounds. A sad horse makes a low whinny. A long neigh means "I feel fine!"

If a horse's ears are back flat, look out! That horse is angry. If a horse bends its ears slightly forward, it is content. If two horses are friends, they rub noses. Would you like to be friends with this wonderful animal?

# Horse Size

Measuring height

The height of a horse is measured in hands. A hand equals four inches. The Belgian draft horse can be as tall as 17 hands. The Arabian horse, which is one of the most beautiful horses, is about 15 hands high.

The Shetland pony is about nine hands high. The smallest horse in the world is the falabella. It is only 12 inches tall!

Belgian

Arabian

Shetland ▶

# Horses & Fun

Horses love to run. A horse runs with joy and often kicks at the wind. Sometimes a mother will have a race with her baby. If a horse cannot run, it gets bored. Horses also like to scratch and rub and roll on the ground.

Horses love company. They like to be around people and other horses and animals. Horses also like to eat!

# Horses & Eating

Horses eat grass, hay, oats, and barley. Oatmeal is good for a tired horse. Never give a small pony too much oatmeal; it makes it too frisky.

Many horses graze, nibbling all day. Some workhorses eat three meals a day. Horses love carrots, apples, molasses, and sugar cubes. A salt block gives the horse important minerals and makes the horse thirsty so it drinks enough water.

# Horses & Sleep

You might have a hard time sleeping standing up. A horse likes to nap this way. Its leg joints lock so it doesn't fall. Horses also lie down to sleep.

Straw or wood shavings make a good bed for a horse. Horses like to sleep in separate stalls, but they like other horses nearby. Baby horses sleep a lot. Sometimes they nap by their mothers.

# Horses' Coats & Colors

Chestnut

Horses come in many colors. Most blacks become rusty blacks, because their coats fade in the sun. Many white horses are born with black coats. As they get older, their coats lighten until they are white. The only true white horse is an albino.

Brown horses with black manes and tails are called bays. Chestnuts are reddish-brown. Sandy bays are light tan.

Bay ▶

# Horses' Coats & Colors

Palomino

Dappled gray

Paint

Some grays have a lot of dark hairs mixed with white. In the old West, this was called a steeldust. A sorrel coat is reddish yellow. A dun is yellow-gray. Palominos are golden. Horses also have patterned coats. The Appaloosa is spotted. Dappled grays have gray patches on their gray coats. Paints have splashes of color.

Which coat is your favorite?

Appaloosa ▶

# Horses & Babies

A baby horse is a foal. Its mother is a mare. Most foals are born in stables. After it is born, a foal is cold, wet, and tired. Soon, it wobbles to its feet. Within a few hours, it runs across the meadow.

During the first weeks of life, the foal drinks its mother's milk. Later, it grazes on grass. The mare and foal are very close.

# Horse Racing

Horse racing in the United States began with the early settlers. An early governor of New York first offered a silver cup to the winner of a race. Racing has been a popular sport since. The best known racehorse is the thoroughbred. Quarter horses are good at short distance races.

The names of a few champions of the past are Man O' War, Citation, and Secretariat.

# Farm Horses

Tractors, trucks, and other farm machinery have replaced farm horses. But the Amish still use horses. The Amish are a religious group that does not believe in using modern machines. Many farmers like the company of workhorses. After all, a tractor isn't friendly and it often won't start in cold weather.

Draft horses are good workers. They have strong bodies and thick muscles. Workhorses often wear blinders so they are not distracted. Draft horses have gentle natures.

# Clydesdale

The Clydesdale (KLYDZ-dayl) is one of the most familiar workhorses. It is a hardy farm animal. In the 1700s, it hauled coal in Scotland. The Clydesdale is an energetic wagon horse.

A team of Clydesdales would have no trouble pulling a heavy wagon filled with autumn pumpkins. This horse is also the fastest of all draft horses.

# Belgian

The most popular draft horse is the powerful Belgian (BEL-juhn). It is also the heaviest workhorse. It is a strong and reliable animal. In weight-pulling contests, Belgian teams almost always win first prize.

For all the work it does, the Belgian doesn't eat a lot. Don't let the size and strength of this horse scare you—the Belgian is calm and gentle.

# Shire

The Shire (SHYRE) is the largest horse. It stands 18 hands or more. This mighty horse may weigh up to a ton. It has the most hair of any breed.

The Shire is slow, but it gets its work done. In old times, the Shire pulled horse-drawn buses. Today it pulls logs and hay.

# Other Workhorses

Besides farming, horses have other jobs. Some horses work the cattle on western ranches, some haul timber, and some march in parades. Police use horses to patrol the streets in some cities. From their tall mounts, police officers can see what is going on.

Other horses pull an old fashioned "cab." Many horses work in movies and TV. Don't forget the horses in the circus.

# Morgan

The first Morgan horse was given to an innkeeper to pay off a debt. This horse is named for that early owner, Justin Morgan. Another name for the Morgan horse is "The Pride of New England."

Many people like this fast, handsome horse for trail riding. The Morgan is sturdy and obedient. Perhaps this is why city police sometimes use the Morgan for patrolling parks and streets, and marching in parades.

# Lippizaner

Did you ever hear of a horse going to a dance class? The Lippizaner (lip-it-SAH-ner) does! At the Spanish Riding School of Vienna in Austria, the Lippizaner learns to dance. It moves and leaps, prances and turns with the grace of a ballerina.

These horses have lovely white coats. They are patient animals and very bright. The Lippizaner's work is to entertain. Don't you think it does its job beautifully?

# Horses for Riding & Recreation

Today, most horses don't have to work hard. But horses are still valued and loved. Riding a horse for fun is called "hacking." People ride horses in competitions. Some even make it to the Olympics. Horses are used to play the game of polo. No matter what its size, a horse in a polo game is called a polo pony.

Horses are fun to watch, especially the daring horses at the rodeo!

# Arabian

The Arabian horse is one of the oldest breeds. Long ago, it was used in the desert by people called bedouins (BED-wuhnz). The Arabian is also one of the most beautiful horses.

It has a fine head and large, pretty eyes. Its high-set tail flows like silk ribbons. These horses are also famous for their speed. The Arabian is smart, gentle, and high-spirited.

# Thoroughbred

Once upon a time there were three Arabian stallions. Every single thoroughbred today can trace its family tree back to one of these stallions. The thoroughbred is the fastest horse of all. It is brave and beautiful. In races, it runs to win.

Thoroughbreds are the celebrities of the horse world. Many have lived in luxury.

# Quarter Horse

The quarter horse is named for the quarter-mile race. It runs this race faster than any other horse. The strong, athletic quarter horse also is an excellent polo pony. At rodeos it is feisty and fun to watch.

The quarter horse also works on many big ranches. It has a talent for working with cattle. The quarter horse is often called the cowboy's horse.

# Ponies

A pony is a special breed of horse that is small. A pony can be no taller than 14.2 hands high. In the past, ponies were hard workers. They helped farmers and ranchers. Some worked in the coal mines.

Queen Victoria of England was very fond of ponies. She used to ride hers through the hills. Ponies make great pets.

Icelandic ponies

New Forest pony ▶

# Shetland

Shetlands (SHET-luhndz) are the most popular ponies. They are rugged and brave and easy to train. The Shetland pony comes from Scotland. In the 1800s, Shetlands were used as "pit ponies." They hauled coal in the mines. Like goats, Shetlands can walk in rocky places.

Shetlands look like tiny draft horses. They come in all colors. Dappled Shetlands always have white manes and tails. Shetlands often perform in circuses.

# Welsh

The people of Wales used the Welsh pony over 2,000 years ago. Because this animal comes from the Welsh hills, it is often called the Welsh mountain pony.

Welsh ponies are gentle and strong. They are very fine jumpers. On snowy country evenings, the Welsh pony may pull a merry sleigh. It may be the most beautiful of all ponies.

# Camargue

The Camargue (kuh-MAYRG) pony is from Camargue in France. It is a very hardy animal. It is used to herd cattle and the black bulls that live in that area.

The Camargue pony is very ancient. They are semiwild. They have rough, brownish coats that lighten to gray when they get older. These ponies also have straight, square faces.

# Horses in the Wild

During the Ice Age, wild horses roamed in herds on every continent except Antarctica. Mustangs (MUHS-tangz) and Assateague/Chincoteague (AS-uh-teeg/shing-kuh-TEEG) horses are semiwild. Their ancestors were tamed. Only the Mongolian (mong-GO-le-uhn) wild horse is truly wild. It comes from primitive times.

Wild horses are hardy. They survive bad weather. They graze on hills, marshes, and grasslands. Today, wild horses are rare. Many people work to keep these animals free and wild.

# Mustang

"Mustang" is the Spanish word for "wild." Mustangs flourished in the West. Many were captured and tamed. Only a few small herds roam wild today. The law protects these beautiful animals.

The mustang played a big part in American history. It was the favorite horse of Native Americans and early ranchers. It also carried the riders of the Pony Express. The mustang is a sturdy and courageous animal.

# Assateague/ Chincoteague

These small, untamed ponies are named for the island on which they live. The island is off the coast of Maryland and Virginia. The ponies are excellent swimmers.

The Assateague/ Chincoteague ponies graze in salt meadows. They eat leaves and berries. In summer, the mosquitoes are pesky, and the ponies roll on the beach to scratch. If that doesn't work, they take a refreshing dip in the ocean.

# Mongolian Wild Horse

Only one horse cannot be tamed—the Mongolian wild horse. It has another name: Przewalski's (pshuh-VAYL-skeez) wild horse. It has changed little since prehistoric times.

Mongolian wild horses have rough, dull yellow coats. In winter, their coats grow shaggy and long. They sometimes have whiskers or beards. During the day, these horses take naps. At night, they move to cool watering places.